Ocean Animals A to Z

A TRACE-THE-LETTER BOOK

by Leslie Falconer

First published by Experience Early Learning Company
7243 Scotchwood Lane, Grawn, Michigan 49637 USA

Text Copyright ©2015 by Experience Early Learning Co.
Printed and Bound in the USA

ISBN 978-1-937954-21-5
visit us at www.ExperienceEarlyLearning.com

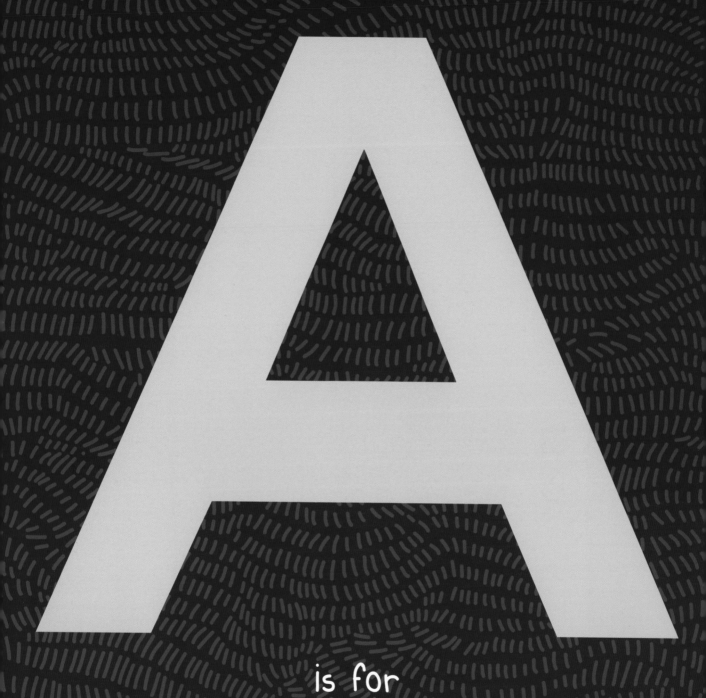

A

is for
angelfish.

Angelfish swim in pairs.

Can you trace the letter A with two fingers?

B

is for
beluga whale.

A beluga whale can swim backwards.

Can you trace the letter B forwards then backwards?

is for
coral.

Corals are made up of many tiny polyps. They look like plants but they are animals.

Can you touch each polyp as you trace the letter C?

D

is for
dolphin.

Dolphins communicate by clicking.

Can you make the /d/ sound over and over

E

is for

eel.

Eels hide under rocks like snakes but they are actually fish.

Can you trace the letter E and then hide your finger under your leg?

is for
fugu.

Fugu can fill up with water and air. This makes them very big!

Can you trace the letter F with your fist?

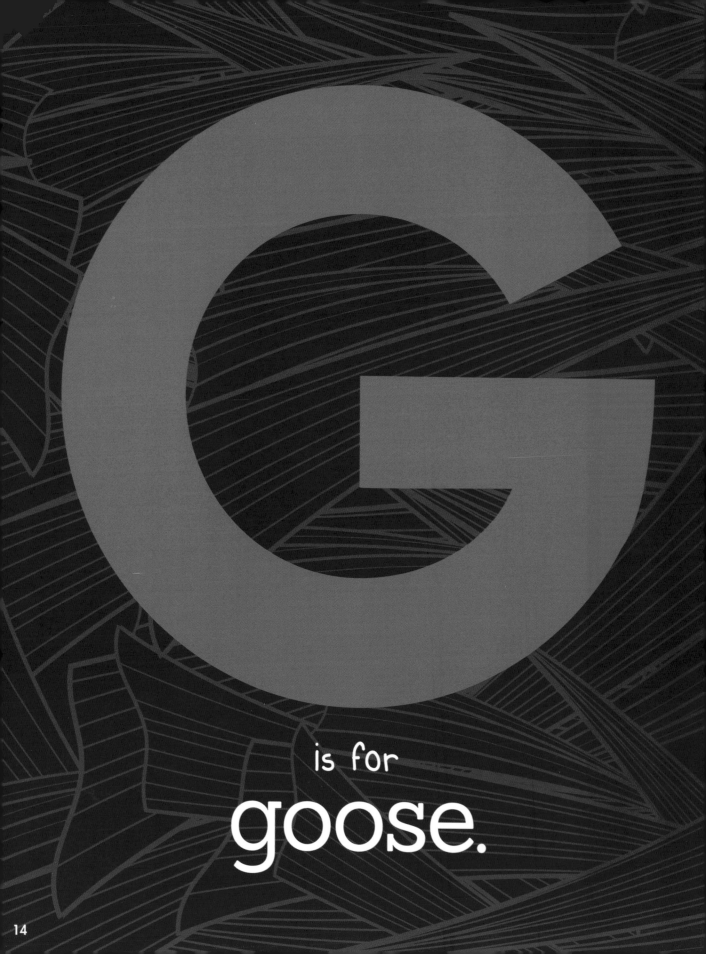

G

is for

goose.

A goose flies and then floats on the ocean waves.

Can you trace the letter G without touching the page?
Fly just above it and then land at the end.

is for
humpback whale.

A humpback whale slaps his flippers and jumps above the water.

Can you jump your finger from the top to the bottom of the H?

I

is for

isopod.

An isopod crawls along the bottom of the ocean and looks like a bug, but it is a crustacean and can grow up to 2 feet long!

Can you crawl your fingers up and down the letter I?

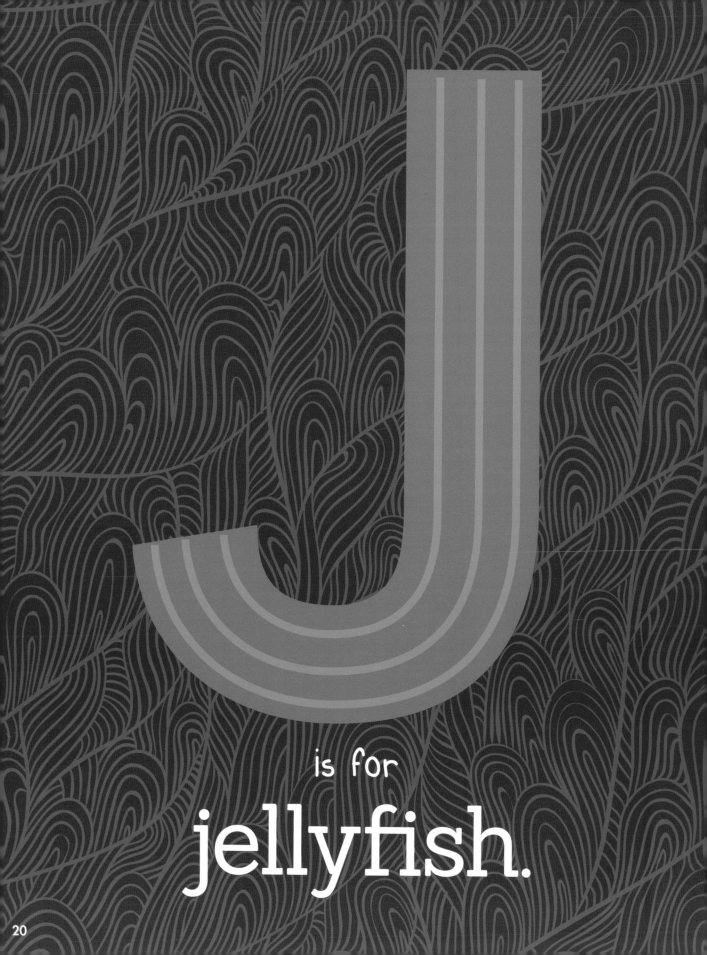

is for
jellyfish.

Jellyfish
tentacles
are very
dangerous.
They sting!

Can you trace the tentacles
on the letter J?

is for

krill.

A krill has a tiny
exoskeleton
and many little legs.

Can you use your pinky finger to trace the letter K?

L

is for
lionfish.

A lionfish has long tentacles that carry poison.

How quickly can you trace the letter L and escape his dangerous sting?

M

is for

manatee.

Manatees are very friendly and very, very slow.

How slowly can you trace the letter M?

is for

narwhal.

A narwhal has a tusk that is actually one long tooth!

Can you trace the letter N with your fingernail?

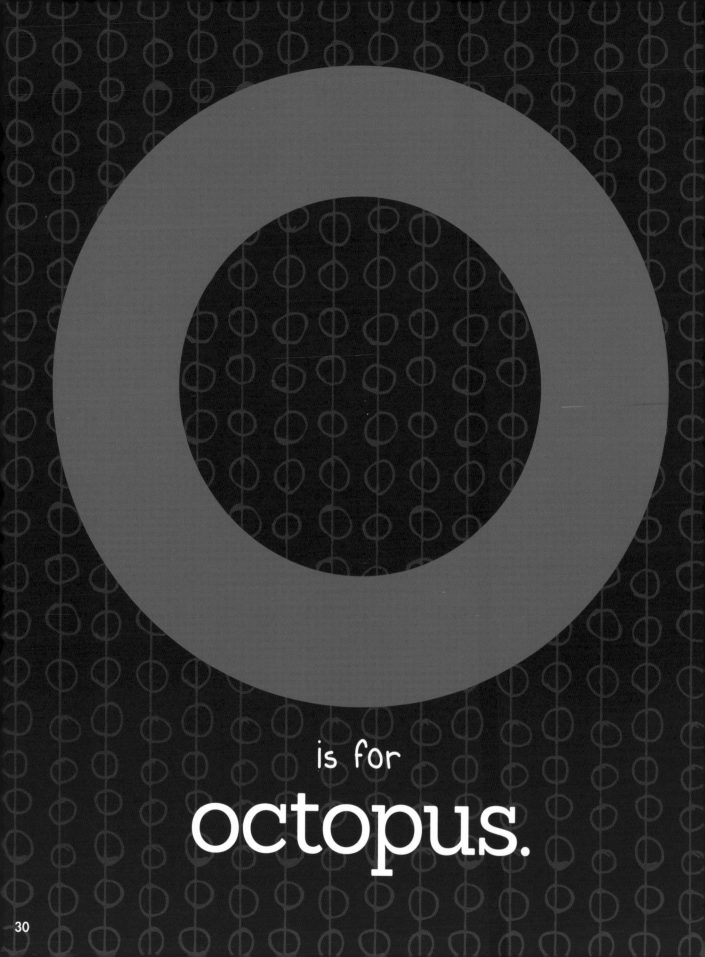

is for
octopus.

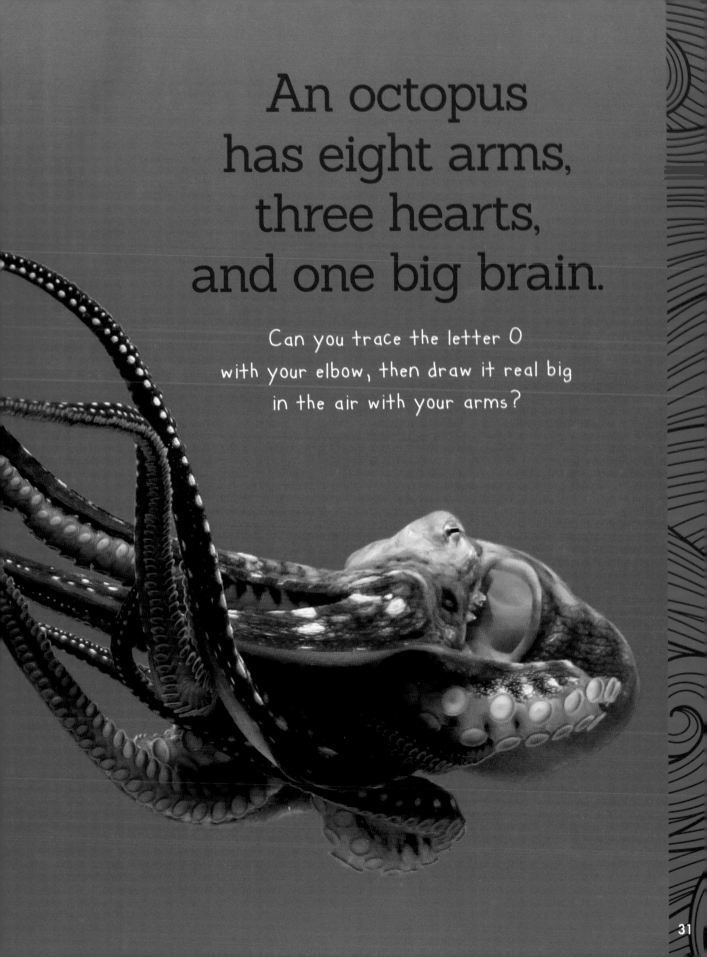

An octopus has eight arms, three hearts, and one big brain.

Can you trace the letter O
with your elbow, then draw it real big
in the air with your arms?

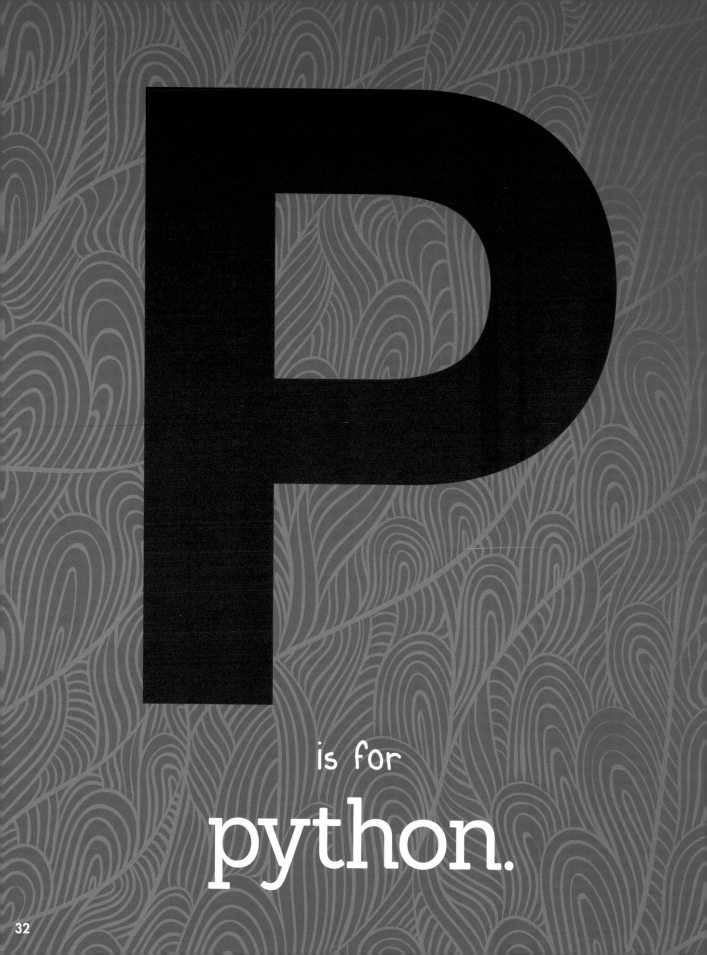

P

is for

python.

A python can live
on land or in sea, but
if it slithers underwater
it must hold its breath.

Can you hold your breath WHILE you trace the letter P?

is for
Queensland grouper.

The Queensland grouper lives in shallow coral reefs. It will attack you if you get too close.

How carefully can you trace the letter Q?
Don't disturb the Queensland grouper!

is for
red waratah anemone.

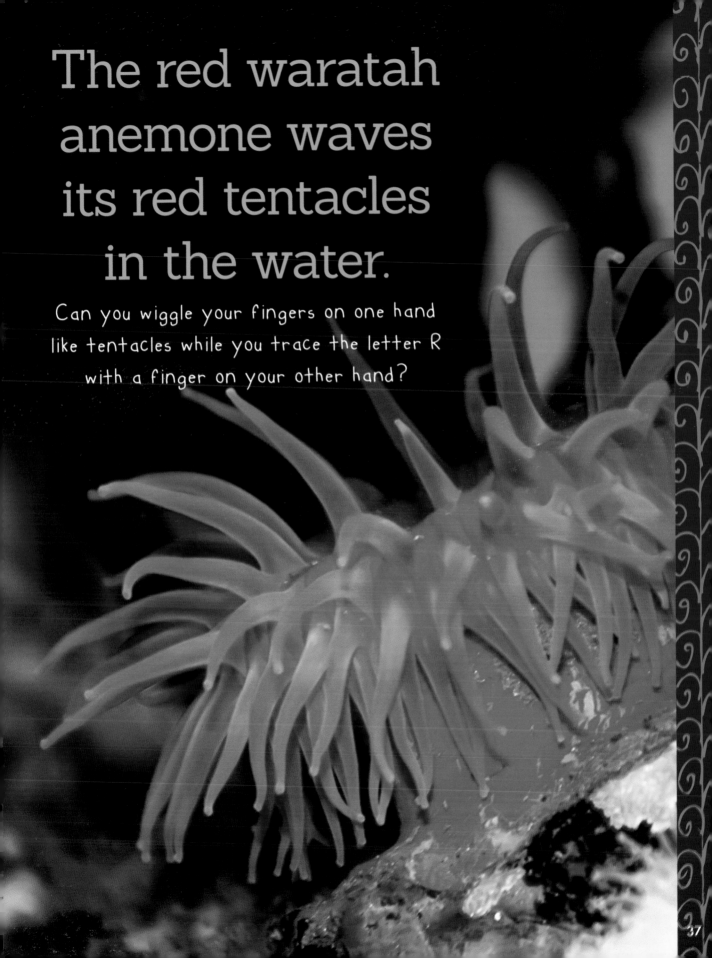

The red waratah anemone waves its red tentacles in the water.

Can you wiggle your fingers on one hand like tentacles while you trace the letter R with a finger on your other hand?

S is for
sea star.

If a sea star is in danger, it will lose an arm. But don't worry, a new one will grow in its place!

Can you trace the letter S with your thumb, then make your thumb disappear?

T

is for
turtle.

A turtle
living
in the ocean
has flippers
instead
of feet.

Can you use your toe
to trace the letter T?

U

is for

unicorn fish.

The unicorn fish has a bony horn on its forehead.

Can you trace the letter U with your nose?

V

is for

volcano sponge.

Volcano sponges
suck in water
and blow it out
through their holes.

Can you trace the letter V
by blowing air on it?

W

is for
walrus.

Walrus have long tusks and a mustache. They snort at their friends.

Can you make a snorting sound while you trace the letter W?

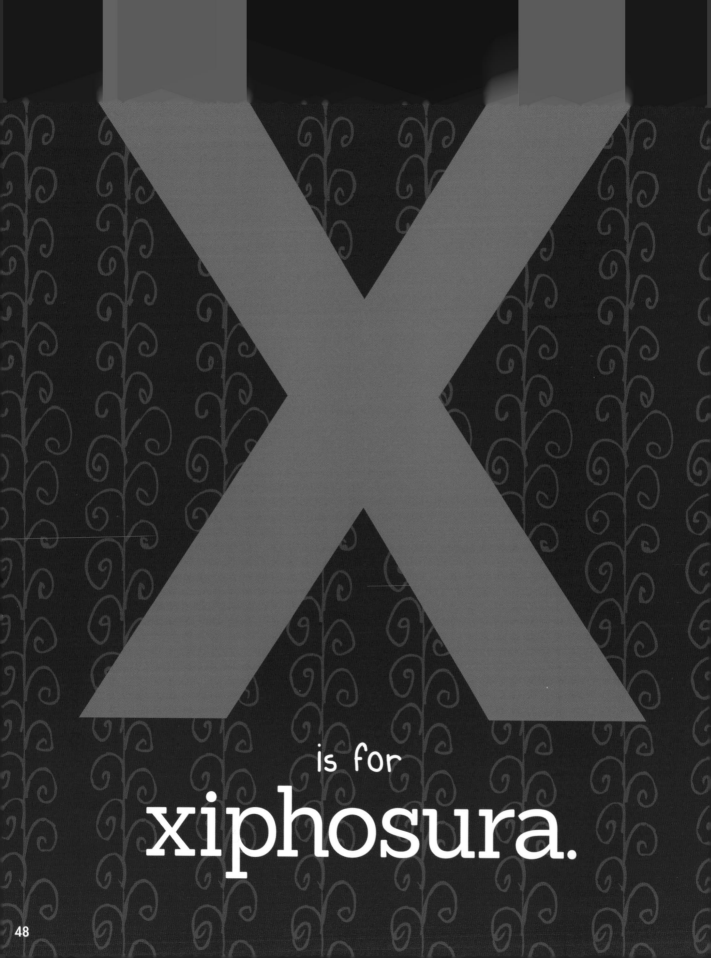

X

is for

xiphosura.

Xiphosura is the Latin name for horseshoe crab. Horseshoe crabs are related to spiders and have 8 legs.

Can you trace the letter X eight times?

Y

is for

yellow tang.

The yellow tang shakes his sharp spine to scare off other fish.

Can you shake your body while you trace the letter Y?

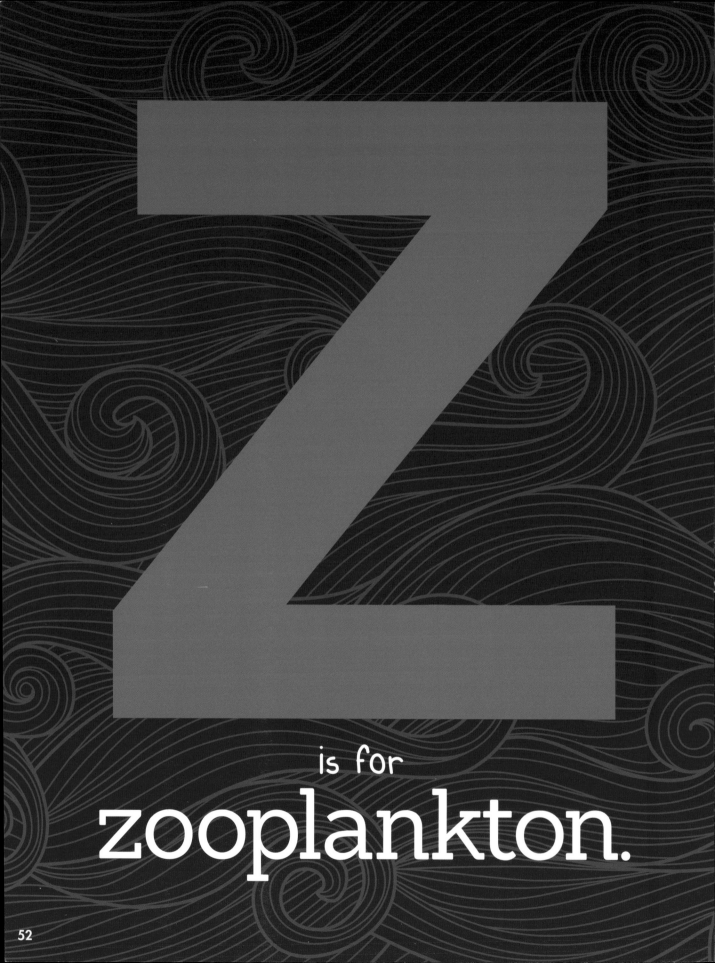

Z
is for
zooplankton.

Zooplankton
are tiny animals
that drift along
the top of the sea.

Can you raise the book and trace
the letter Z above your head?

Ocean animals A to Z!

Can you trace and name them all?

Experience Early Learning specializes in the development and publishing
of research-based curriculum, books, music and authentic assessment
tools for early childhood teachers and parents around the world.
Our mission is to inspire children to experience learning through creative
expression, play and open-ended discovery. We believe educational
materials that invite children to participate with their whole self
(mind, body and spirit) support on-going development and encourage
children to become the authors of their own unique learning stories.

www.ExperienceEarlyLearning.com